BASEBALL
STATS
AND THE STORIES BEHIND THEM

What Every Fan Needs to Know

by Eric Braun

CAPSTONE PRESS
a capstone imprint

Sports Illustrated Kids Stats & Stories are published by Capstone Press,
1710 Roe Crest Drive, North Mankato, Minnesota 56003.
www.mycapstone.com

Library of Congress Cataloging-in-Publication Data
is available on the Library of Congress website.
ISBN 978-1-4914-8215-5 (library binding)
ISBN 978-1-4914-8584-2 (paperback)
ISBN 978-1-4914-8588-0 (eBook PDF)

Editorial Credits
Nick Healy, editor; Ted Williams, designer; Eric Gohl, media researcher;
Tori Abraham, production specialist

Photo Credits
Library of Congress: 9 (right), 10, 35, 44 (bottom), 45; Newscom: Icon SMI/Andrew
Dieb, 24, 27, Icon SMI/Gary Rothstein, 20, Icon SMI/John Rivera, 9 (left), MCT/
Ron Jenkins, 25, ZUMA Press/TSN, 15, ZUMA Press/Will Vragovic, 30–31; Sports
Illustrated: Al Tielemans, 14 (bottom), 17, Chuck Solomon, 16, 19, 44 (top), David E.
Klutho, 13, 29, Hy Peskin, 5, 8, John Biever, 14 (top), 18, 38, John Iacono, 43, John W.
McDonough, cover, 1, 42, Manny Millan, 41, Robert Beck, 6, 21 (top), 22, 23, 37, Simon
Bruty, 34, V.J. Lovero, 12, 21 (bottom), 32

Editor's Note
All statistics are through the 2014 MLB season unless otherwise noted.

Printed in the United States of America in North Mankato, Minnesota.
112015   009221CGS16

TABLE OF CONTENTS

Statistics are to the game of baseball what those familiar red stitches are to an actual baseball. Stats help us get a grip on every game, every play, every player. Baseball wouldn't look the same without them.

It has been this way almost since the beginning. As early as 1837, baseball-playing Americans in Philadelphia made a rule that all games had to be recorded in a book. The record book would include how many outs each player made and how many times he scored.

On October 22, 1845, the first baseball box score appeared in the *New York Morning News*. A simple and elegant summary of what happened in a ballgame, the box score allowed fans who didn't attend the game to quickly catch up on what they missed. As box scores grew more complex over the years, readers could measure just how players performed in various parts of the game.

In 1861 a reporter named Henry Chadwick began publishing an annual guide to the game called *Beadle's Dime Base-Ball Player*. In it he recapped the sport's best teams and players from the previous year and reported players' stats.

Baseball fans loved to read those stats. Even practice games were thoroughly reported in newspapers. Reporters worked to invent more stats so that fans could evaluate the game in even more detail. Stats became so important, some fans and journalists complained that players cared more about their numbers than their team's success. (We can sometimes hear these same complaints today!)

Just like the stats, the game itself was evolving during the 1800s too. For example, pitchers originally tossed the ball underhand and weren't allowed to try to fool the batter. Fielders didn't use gloves. But by 1900, baseball looked mostly like the game we know today. And many of the stats used to understand the game looked a lot like the stats we see now: earned run average, batting average, errors.

Some of those stats are famous, like Hall-of-Famer Ted Williams' 1941 batting average (.406). Some of them mean very little, like little-known Eric Cammack's lifetime slugging percentage of 3.000. But every one of them tells a story about the game. Like stitches on a baseball, they bind the sport together and help make it what it is.

CHAPTER 1
BATTING AVERAGE

No baseball stat is more familiar than batting average. It's one of the oldest stats in the game, officially used for the first time in 1876. And it gives a quick snapshot of a player's hitting ability.

Batting average is also simple. You just take the number of hits a player gets and divide it by the number of at bats. The answer you get is a decimal that's usually displayed to the third digit. For example, in 2014 Detroit Tigers designated hitter Victor Martinez got **188** hits out of **561** at bats.

$$188 \div 561 = .335$$

That's a very good average—second best in the American League (AL) that year.

▶ VICTOR MARTINEZ

EARNING THE TITLE

If Victor Martinez's .335 batting average was only second best in 2014, who had the best? That would be Houston Astros second baseman Jose Altuve. But he wasn't sure to win the AL batting title until the last day of the season.

Back up: Two days before the end of the season, Altuve had a slight lead over Martinez. But he went 0 for 4, lowering his average to .340. That same day, Martinez went 1 for 2 and raised his average to .337 in his game against the Minnesota Twins. Astros general manager Jeff Luhnow wanted to protect his star second baseman from dropping his average even further. The Astros announced that Altuve would be benched for the last game.

But Altuve didn't want to win the title that way, and he told Luhnow so. At the last minute, the team reversed its decision and let him play. Altuve rewarded them—and himself—by going 2 for 4 to raise his average to .341. Over in Minnesota, Martinez went 0 for 4, dropping his average to .335.

Celebrating after the game, Altuve explained his decision. "I think this is way better than just sitting on the bench and waiting for something. If you want to win something, you've got to win it on the field."

TO HIT .400

Back in 1941, legendary hitter Ted Williams made a similar decision. For him, the batting title was not on the line—he had that wrapped up by a mile. But he had a chance to finish the season hitting over .400. Only a handful of the greatest hitters of all time have done that.

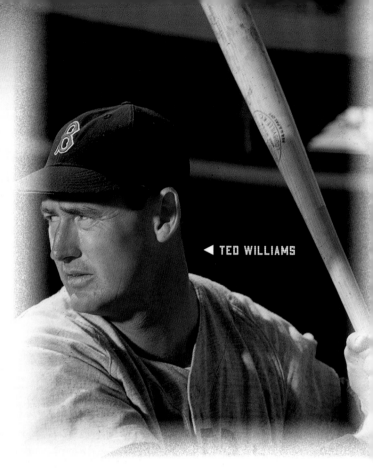

◄ TED WILLIAMS

Williams was hitting .401 with three games to go. His Boston Red Sox and their opponents, the Philadelphia Athletics, had no chance to make the postseason. With nothing on the line, the Red Sox manager suggested that Williams sit out to protect his average.

But Williams wanted to play. He went 1 for 4 in the Saturday game, which dropped him to .39955. Going into a doubleheader on Sunday, Williams was nervous. But he got a sharp single in his first at bat and went on to go 4 for 5 in the first game—including a home run. That raised his average to .404. But Williams wasn't done. He went 2 for 4 in the afternoon game, finishing at .406.

Nobody has hit .400 or over since.

TOP BATTING AVERAGES, 2014

▲ JOSE ALTUVE

Name	Team	AVG
AMERICAN LEAGUE		
JOSE ALTUVE	ASTROS	.341
VICTOR MARTINEZ	TIGERS	.335
MICHAEL BRANTLEY	INDIANS	.327
NATIONAL LEAGUE		
JUSTIN MORNEAU	ROCKIES	.319
JOSH HARRISON	PIRATES	.315
ANDREW MCCUTCHEN	PIRATES	.314

BEST CAREER BATTING AVERAGES
Minimum 1,000 games played

▲ TY COBB

Name	Team	AVG
TY COBB	TIGERS/ATHLETICS	.366 (.36636)
ROGERS HORNSBY	CARDINALS/CUBS/GIANTS/BRAVES/BROWNS	.358 (.35850)
JOE JACKSON	WHITE SOX/NAPS/INDIANS/ATHLETICS	.356 (.35575)
ED DELAHANTY	PHILLIES/SENATORS/QUAKERS/INFANTS	.346 (.34590)
TRIS SPEAKER	INDIANS/RED SOX/SENATORS/ATHLETICS/AMERICANS	.345 (.34468)
TED WILLIAMS	RED SOX	.344 (.34441)
BILLY HAMILTON	PHILLIES/BEANEATERS/COWBOYS	.344 (.34429)
BABE RUTH	YANKEES/RED SOX/BRAVES	.342 (.34206)
HARRY HEILMANN	TIGERS/REDS	.342 (.34159)
PETE BROWNING	COLONELS/ECLIPSE/REDS/INFANTS/PIRATES/BROWNS/BRIDEGROOMS	.341 (.34149)

◀ BABE RUTH

It's a homer. A bomb. A blast. A tater. A moonshot. Four-bagger. Round-tripper. He parked it. He tattooed it. He went deep. Went yard. That one's not coming back.

Everyone loves a home run. Everyone except the pitcher, that is. They're fun to watch, and they're fun to talk about.

SLUGGERS AND CONTROVERSY

Babe Ruth was the original home run slugger. A big man with a big personality, he held the records for most home runs in a season (60) and in a career (714) for decades. In 1961 Roger Maris of the New York Yankees hit his 61st home run on the last day of the season. That broke Ruth's 34-year-old record.

Maris' feat was controversial, though. That year the league had expanded the schedule to 162 games. Before that, teams played only 154. Some argued that in order for Maris to "truly" break the record, he would have to do it in 154 games like Ruth did. But the record stood and wasn't bested until Mark McGwire hit 70 in 1998.

STEROID ERA

From roughly the late 1980s to the late 2000s, the use of performance-enhancing drugs (PEDs) was widespread in baseball. This led to unprecedented offense—especially home runs. Because PEDs were against the rules, many people now consider the home run records set during that time to be illegitimate, or not the true records. Barry Bonds is the all-time home run king with 762 career bombs, though many call Hank Aaron's 755 the "true" record.

Major League Baseball (MLB) started testing for PEDs in 2005, and since then offense has gone down. Teams averaged 0.86 home runs per game in 2014, down from a peak of 1.17 per game in 2000. In 2000, 16 players hit 40 or more home runs. In 2014, only one player did.

▶ BARRY BONDS

► MARK McGWIRE

MOST HOME RUNS IN A SINGLE SEASON

Rank	Player	HR	Year	Team
1.	BARRY BONDS	73	2001	GIANTS
2.	MARK McGWIRE	70	1998	CARDINALS
3.	SAMMY SOSA	66	1998	CUBS
4.	MARK McGWIRE	65	1999	CARDINALS
5.	SAMMY SOSA	64	2001	CUBS
6.	SAMMY SOSA	63	1999	CUBS
7.	ROGER MARIS	61	1961	YANKEES
8.	BABE RUTH	60	1927	YANKEES
9.	BABE RUTH	59	1921	YANKEES
10.	JIMMIE FOXX	58	1932	ATHLETICS

CHAPTER 3

RUNS BATTED IN

In 2006 Ryan Howard led both leagues in RBIs, or runs batted in, with 149. That means that when he came up to bat with teammates on base, he "batted them in" to score. The hulking first baseman was such a good hitter with runners on base that he led the league in RBIs again in 2008, with 146, and again in 2009, with 141.

▲ RYAN HOWARD

Howard was lucky to have two effective "table-setters," Shane Victorino and Chase Utley, batting before him in the lineup. If his teammates weren't so good at getting on base, he would have had a lot fewer RBIs. In a way, an RBI is a measure of a team's success as much as it is a measure of one player's ability.

▶ CHASE UTLEY

Even so, it takes a lot of skill and steely nerves to get the big hits when the pressure is on. A look at the RBI leaders through history features some of the most fearsome hitters of all time. All but one of these players are in the Baseball Hall of Fame.

BEST SINGLE-SEASON RBI TOTALS

Rank	Player	RBIs	Season
1.	HACK WILSON	191	1930
2.	LOU GEHRIG	185	1931
3.	HANK GREENBERG	184	1937
4.	JIMMIE FOXX	175	1938
5.	LOU GEHRIG	173	1927
	LOU GEHRIG	173	1930
7.	CHUCK KLEIN	170	1930
8.	JIMMIE FOXX	169	1932
9.	HANK GREENBERG	168	1935
	BABE RUTH	168	1921

▲ LOU GEHRIG

BATTED IN?

Getting a hit is the most common way to pick up an RBI, but a bases-loaded walk will also drive in a run, as will getting hit by a pitch. A sacrifice fly or bunt will also do the trick.

CHAPTER 4

ON-BASE PERCENTAGE

Flame-throwing pitchers and power hitters get most of the headlines, but you can't win a baseball game without scoring runs. The guys who get on base most are sometimes known as the "sparkplugs" because they spark the offense. These guys aren't always flashy, but their high on-base percentage (OBP) is the key to scoring runs.

On-base percentage is just what it sounds like: the percentage of times that a batter gets on base. Like batting average, it is expressed as a three-digit decimal. If you come to bat ten times and get on base four times, you have an OBP of .400. But unlike batting average, OBP gives batters credit for getting on base any way they do it—including by walk.

▶ JASON GIAMBI

OBP VALUE

OBP was not always valued very highly by baseball people. More traditional statistics such as batting average and stolen bases were considered more important. That changed in the late 1990s and early 2000s when the Oakland Athletics began assembling teams made up of high-OBP players who didn't necessarily have great traditional statistics.

Because their traditional stats were less impressive, these players were less expensive to sign. By seeking out such bargains, the A's were able to assemble competitive teams with less money than big-market teams, such as those in New York and Los Angeles. Jason Giambi, one of the A's stars, led the American League in OBP in 2000 and 2001. Despite its relatively tiny payroll, the team went to the playoffs in 2002 and 2003.

BEST SINGLE-SEASON OBPs

Rank	Player	OBP	Year
1.	BARRY BONDS	.6094	2004
2.	BARRY BONDS	.5817	2002
3.	TED WILLIAMS	.5528	1941
4.	JOHN MCGRAW	.5475	1899
5.	BABE RUTH	.5445	1923

▲ BARRY BONDS

OBP SKILL

A batter with a good eye knows when to let close pitches go for balls. He can also foul off tough strikes, forcing the pitcher to throw more pitches. That increases the chance that the pitcher will throw balls.

Speed plays an important role in OBP as well. A fast runner can turn infield grounders into hits by beating out throws to first. These speedsters put pressure on the defense.

Take a look at the following table. It lists the players with the ten best batting averages in the American League in 2014. It also shows how many runs they scored.

HIGHEST BA 2014, AMERICAN LEAGUE

Rank	Name	Team	Runs	AVG
1.	JOSE ALTUVE	ASTROS	85	.341
2.	VICTOR MARTINEZ	TIGERS	87	.335
3.	MICHAEL BRANTLEY	INDIANS	94	.327
4.	ADRIAN BELTRE	RANGERS	79	.324
5.	JOSE ABREU	WHITE SOX	80	.317

▲ MICHAEL BRANTLEY

Minnesota second baseman Brian Dozier batted .242 that year, which is nowhere near the top ten in the AL. But he walked 89 times, lifting his OBP to .345. Because of his skill at getting on base, he scored 112 runs— second most in baseball.

HIT BY PITCH

One less common—and more painful—way of getting on base is to be hit by a pitch (HBP). Some batters actually have a skill for this! Hall-of-Famer Craig Biggio was hit by 285 pitches in his career, good for second-most all time. He led the league in HBP five times over his 20 years in the game. He also had a very good career OBP of .363.

◀ CRAIG BIGGIO

CHAPTER 5

SLUGGING PERCENTAGE

In 2000 Mets reliever Eric Cammack came up to bat and hit a triple. Since relief pitchers almost never bat, that ended up being his only career trip to the plate. When he retired, he had a career slugging percentage of 3.000—right at the top of the record books for that stat.

Slugging percentage (SLG) is a measure of a hitter's power. To figure it out, you divide the player's total bases by the number of at bats.

For example, let's say you come up to bat 100 times in a season. You hit 20 singles, 6 doubles, 1 triple, and 3 home runs. *Add up all those bases:*

20 singles x 1 base each = 20
6 doubles x 2 bases each = 12
1 triple x 3 bases each = 3
3 home runs x 4 bases each = 12
Total bases = 47

Divide your total bases **(47)** by your total at bats **(100)**.

47 ÷ 100 = .470 SLG

▶ ERIC CAMMACK

So if Cammack had a career SLG of 3.000, why haven't we heard more about this amazing hitter? The answer, of course, is that he only batted once. The best hitters keep hitting for extra bases time and time again—not just once. When Miguel Cabrera slugged .636 for the 2013 season, it helped earn him a second consecutive MVP award.

▲ MIGUEL CABRERA

CAREER SLUGGING PERCENTAGE LEADERS
Minimum of 3,000 plate appearances

Rank	Player	Slugging %
1.	BABE RUTH	.6897
2.	TED WILLIAMS	.6338
3.	LOU GEHRIG	.6324
4.	JIMMIE FOXX	.6093
5.	BARRY BONDS	.6069
6.	HANK GREENBERG	.6050
7.	MARK McGWIRE	.5882
8.	ALBERT PUJOLS	.5861
9.	MANNY RAMIREZ	.5854
10.	JOE DIMAGGIO	.5788

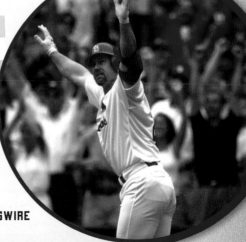

▶ MARK McGWIRE

CHAPTER 6

ON-BASE PLUS SLUGGING PERCENTAGE

Some baseball statistics seek to measure very specific parts of the game. How well a player hits versus left-handed pitchers. The speed of a pitcher's fastball. How often a catcher throws out would-be base-stealers.

But sometimes you want a single stat that gives a big picture. For hitters, one such stat is on-base plus slugging percentage (OPS). OPS measures a hitter's ability to get on base and hit for power—the two main hitting skills. It's simple to calculate—just add the player's OBP and his SLG.

When Miguel Cabrera won the MVP in 2013, he had a .636 SLG and a .442 OBP, giving him an OPS of 1.078 (.636 + .442). Mike Trout had an OPS of .988 that year and came in second for the MVP voting. Cabrera also played for a winning team in Detroit, while Trout's Angels had a losing record that year.

Some analysts thought Trout should have won the MVP even though his OPS was lower. He was an elite defender at one of the toughest positions, center field. Cabrera was a mediocre defender at the easiest position, first base. In the end, it was hard for voters to ignore Cabrera's huge offensive year.

BEST CAREER OPS
Top five all time

Rank	Player	OPS
1.	BABE RUTH	1.1636
2.	TED WILLIAMS	1.1155
3.	LOU GEHRIG	1.0798
4.	BARRY BONDS	1.0512
5.	JIMMIE FOXX	1.0376

BEST CAREER OPS, ACTIVE PLAYERS
Top five active players, minimum 3,000 plate appearances

Rank	Player	OPS
1.	ALBERT PUJOLS	.5861
2.	MIGUEL CABRERA	.5636
3.	ALEX RODRIGUEZ	.5575
4.	RYAN BRAUN	.5484
5.	DAVID ORTIZ	.5423

▲ ALBERT PUJOLS

CHAPTER 7
ERRORS AND FIELDING PERCENTAGE

Early in the 2014 season, Yu Darvish of the Texas Rangers was pitching a gem. He had a no-hitter going in the seventh inning when David Ortiz dropped a looping drive into shallow right field. Texas second baseman Rougned Odor ran back. The right fielder, Alex Rios, ran in. But neither of them came up with the ball. It looked like a clean hit, but the official scorer for the game called it an error on Rios.

In another situation, it might not matter much. Darvish got out of the inning without allowing a run—no harm done. But the decision meant that Darvish's no-hitter was still alive. Many people thought it was clearly a hit. They believed the scorekeeper called it an error for a reason: to preserve the no-hitter for Darvish. Later in the game, Darvish gave up a hit anyway.

▶ YU DARVISH

► ALEX RIOS

◄ ROUGNED ODOR

SHOULDA GOT IT!

Baseball has long used "errors" to measure defensive ability. The idea, basically, is this: If the official scorer thinks the defender should have made a play that he didn't, that defender is given an error. You can divide a player's errors by the number of "chances" he had—or balls hit that he should have fielded—and you arrive at his fielding percentage.

One problem with this system is that sometimes it's not so obvious if the player should have made a play. Bias can also influence decisions. In other words, a scorer's judgment is not always perfect.

Sometimes decisions about errors can get really messy. For example, about a week after the Darvish near no-hitter, Major League Baseball made the unusual decision to change the scorer's call. Ortiz was given a single in the seventh inning, and Rios' error was erased. Apparently the league felt the scorer made the wrong choice.

Would MLB have made that change if Darvish had completed the game without giving up any other hits? He and his teammates would have celebrated the "no-no" on the field. T-shirts and baseballs commemorating the event would have been sold. It would have been hard to change after all that.

ANOTHER DISPUTE, ANOTHER HIT

About a month after the Darvish game, David Ortiz was involved in another controversy over one of his hits. He smashed a grounder toward first base, where Twins first baseman Joe Mauer knocked it down while falling to his knees. The Twins failed to get an out, and the scorekeeper gave Mauer an error. Ortiz argued that it should have been a hit. Mauer had made a great play to even come close to getting an out. Once again, MLB later agreed with Ortiz and changed it to a hit.

CHAPTER 8

ULTIMATE ZONE RATING

What about a fielder who has great range and gets to more balls than other players? Counting errors doesn't tell us how much that player is helping his team by making outs that other players simply can't.

POSTSEASON HERO

Kansas City Royals center fielder Lorenzo Cain is a great example of such a player. Royals fans have known for a long time how good he is, and in the 2014 postseason he showed off his skills to a national audience. Cain flew all over the field, gobbling up fly balls that other outfielders wouldn't get close to. He made diving catches. Sliding catches. He leapt above the wall in center field to take away homers. He sprinted across the outfield at blazing speeds to rob batters of hits.

One way to get a better picture of a defender's value is with a stat called ultimate zone rating (UZR). The UZR system divides the field into zones and looks at all the plays a fielder makes—and doesn't make—in the zones. This information is then compared to years of historical data to find out how the player compares to an "average" player at his position. Players get more credit for catches made in zones farther from their initial position.

◄ LORENZO CAIN

UZR is very complicated to compute, but it's easy to understand. It is expressed as a number of runs saved or lost. Lorenzo Cain had a UZR of 10.1 for the 2014 season. That means he saved his team 10.1 runs compared to the average center fielder.

Other defenders with impressive UZRs include Tampa Bay Rays center fielder Kevin Kiermaier. With his tremendous range and powerful arm, he compiled a jaw-dropping UZR of 30.0 in 2015. Also in 2015, shortstop Andrelton Simmons produced a 17.3 UZR for the Atlanta Braves. That number was tops among all infielders that season.

▶ KEVIN KIERMAIER

UZR IN CONTEXT

The baseball statistics website Fangraphs.com breaks down how to understand a player's UZR this way:

DEFENSIVE ABILITY	UZR
GOLD GLOVE CALIBER	+15
GREAT	+10
ABOVE AVERAGE	+5
AVERAGE	0
BELOW AVERAGE	-5
POOR	-10
AWFUL	-15

CHAPTER 9

EARNED RUN AVERAGE

Perhaps the most dominant pitcher of all time was Pedro Martinez. Pedro thrived as a strikeout menace during the steroid era, when offense ruled (see page 12). While most players of the time were bulky and strong, Pedro stood 5 feet 11 inches and weighed only 170 pounds. Yet during his 18-year career he struck out 3,154 batters, at a rate of 10.0 per nine innings. Sometimes he fooled hitters. Sometimes he overpowered them. Either way he was dominant.

Pedro won the Cy Young Award, given to the league's best pitcher, three times, and he was the runner-up twice. But one of the easiest ways to tell how great he was is to look at his earned run average (ERA). ERA is the average number of earned runs a pitcher gives up over nine innings, the length of a game. To find a pitcher's ERA, you divide the number of earned runs allowed by the number of innings pitched and multiply by nine. (Get out your calculator!)

PEDRO MARTINEZ CAREER

919 earned runs
2827 1/3 innings
919 ÷ 2827 1/3 = .32504
0.32504 x 9 = 2.93 ERA

That means that for every nine innings, Pedro gave up less than three earned runs on average. In his best season, 1999, he pitched 213 1/3 innings and gave up 49 earned runs for an ERA of 2.07. The average ERA that year was nearly three runs higher, at 4.70.

TOP CAREER ERAs
Minimum of 1,000 innings pitched

Rank	Player	Team	Year	ERA
1.	ED WALSH	WHITE SOX, BRAVES	1904–1917	1.816
2.	ADDIE JOSS	NAPS, BRONCHOS	1902–1910	1.887
3.	JIM DEVLIN	GRAYS, WHITE STOCKINGS, WHITES	1873–1877	1.896
4.	JACK PFIESTER	CUBS, PIRATES	1903–1911	2.024
5.	SMOKY JOE WOOD	RED SOX, INDIANS	1908–1922	2.033

BEST SINGLE-SEASON ERAs IN HISTORY

Rank	Player	Team	ERA	Year
1.	TIM KEEFE	TROJANS	0.857	1880
2.	DUTCH LEONARD	RED SOX	0.961	1914
3.	MORDECAI BROWN	CUBS	1.038	1906
4.	BOB GIBSON	CARDINALS	1.123	1968
5.	CHRISTY MATHEWSON	GIANTS	1.144	1909

EARNED vs. UNEARNED

Runs that score due to an error by the defense are not considered "earned" by the batter, so they don't count against a pitcher's ERA.

◀ MARIANO RIVERA

Many faithful baseball fans today pay close attention to a pitcher's WHIP. The name stands for "walks plus hits per inning pitched." Invented in 1979 by writer and baseball fanatic Dan Okrent, WHIP is a good way to look deeper than ERA at a pitcher's performance. The stat is basically the average number of batters a pitcher allows on base per inning.

This list contains some of the greatest pitchers in history, including Yankees reliever Mariano Rivera, who retired in 2013.

▶ ADDIE JOSS

BEST CAREER WHIPS
Minimum of 1,000 innings pitched

Rank	Player	Team	Year	WHIP
1.	ADDIE JOSS	NAPS/BRONCHOS	1902–1910	0.9678
2.	ED WALSH	WHITE SOX/BRAVES	1904–1917	0.9996
3.	MARIANO RIVERA	YANKEES	1995–2013	1.0003
4.	JOHN WARD	GIANTS/GRAYS/BRIDEGROOMS/GOTHAMS/WARD'S WONDERS	1878–1894	1.0544
5.	PEDRO MARTINEZ	RED SOX/EXPOS/METS/DODGERS/PHILLIES	1992–2009	1.0544

RELIEF ADVANTAGE

Statistics tell us it's harder for pitchers to get batters out when they face them multiple times in a game. Batters get a little more comfortable with the pitcher each time they go to the plate. That explains the fact that relief pitchers typically have a much better WHIP than starting pitchers. Relievers face only a few batters a game, and they almost never face an entire lineup.

Of the top 10 pitchers in WHIP in 2014, only one was a starter—Clayton Kershaw of the Dodgers.

2014 WHIP LEADERS
Minimum of 60 innings pitched

Rank	Player	Team	Innings Pitched	WHIP	ERA
1.	SEAN DOOLITTLE	A'S	62.2	0.73	2.73
2.	DELLIN BETANCES	YANKEES	90.0	0.78	1.40
3.	PAT NESHEK	CARDINALS	67.1	0.79	1.87
4.	ANDREW MILLER	ORIOLES/ RED SOX	62.1	0.80	2.02
	JOE SMITH	ANGELS	74.2	0.80	1.81
6.	MICHAEL PINEDA	YANKEES	76.1	0.83	1.89
7.	BRAD BOXBERGER	RAYS	64.2	0.84	2.37
8.	WADE DAVIS	ROYALS	72.0	0.85	1.00
9.	CLAYTON KERSHAW	DODGERS	198.1	0.86	1.77
10.	MARK MELANCON	PIRATES	71.0	0.87	1.90

◄ CLAYTON KERSHAW

CHAPTER 11

FIELDING-INDEPENDENT PITCHING

Oh, those poor Detroit pitchers. On paper, the Tigers of the early 2010s had one of the best starting rotations in all baseball. But their ERA was consistently in the bottom half of the league. What happened?

Pitchers don't control everything that happens when they're pitching. Have you ever seen a pitcher get the batter to hit an easy grounder, but the infield can't turn it into an out? Some fielders are really good at making outs on balls in play. Others are not as good. Luck plays a role too.

A NEW STAT

In the late 1990s, a baseball writer named Robert "Voros" McCracken began thinking about how fans and teams evaluate pitchers. He believed that things pitchers do not control—almost everything that happens after a ball is struck by a batter—have a huge effect on scoring. To find out how good a pitcher really is, you have to strip away those things that he doesn't affect directly. McCracken wanted a stat that measures only things the pitcher can control.

In 2001 he published a ground-breaking article online in which he laid out his ideas about "defense-independent pitching" statistics. A few mainstream media members picked up on McCracken's article, including Rob Neyer of ESPN.com. Not long after that, another baseball thinker who goes by the name TangoTiger invented fielding-independent pitching (FIP).

PITCHERS' SKILLS

FIP measures a pitcher's skills based on strikeouts, walks, and home runs. Strikeouts are good. Walks and home runs are not.

FIP looks at how many of those three outcomes a pitcher allows per inning and spits out a number that looks like ERA. You can read it the same way. FIP is like a pitcher's ERA if he had received league average defense and luck.

The 2012 Detroit starting pitchers had a FIP of 3.56. That was third best in all baseball, but their ERA was 3.76. In other words, the Tigers defense was costing the team an average of .20 of a run every game. Things didn't get better the next couple years.

The Tigers' 2013 FIP of 3.12 was the best in MLB, while their 3.38 FIP in 2014 was third-best. The Tigers' ERAs in both cases were middle of the pack.

TIGERS STARTING PITCHERS

Year	FIP	ERA
2012	3.56	3.76
2013	3.12	3.44
2014	3.38	3.89

STRIKEOUTS

Strikeouts. They're at the core of baseball. They're so important, we sing about them during the seventh inning stretch: "It's one, two, three strikes you're out!"

When a pitcher strikes out a batter, it's a show of power and dominance. He doesn't need help from his defense. The batter can't even put the ball in play.

GIVE A LITTLE, GET A LITTLE

If a hitter strikes out too often, he isn't helping his team. So hitters who strike out a lot may soon find themselves on the bench. However, there is an exception to this rule. Think about a player who hits the ball really hard. He tends to get a lot of extra-base hits, like home runs, when he does make contact. Most teams are willing to live with the strikeouts if they know the hitter will bash more homers.

Houston outfielder Chris Carter is an example of this kind of player. He struck out 182 times in 2014, but he also hit 37 bombs.

STRIKEOUT RATE

If you divide the number of times a hitter strikes out by his number of at bats, you get his strikeout rate (or K rate). Outfielder Ben Revere strikes out very rarely compared to other major leaguers. Playing for the Phillies in 2014, he whiffed only 49 times in 601 at bats, giving him a strikeout rate of about 8 percent.

◄ NOLAN RYAN

K RATE IN CONTEXT

Here's a rough guide for understanding K rates, according to the baseball stats analysts at Fangraphs.com.

EXCELLENT	10%
GREAT	12.5%
ABOVE AVERAGE	16%
AVERAGE	20%
BELOW AVERAGE	22%
POOR	25%
AWFUL	27.5%

STRIKEOUTS RISE

▼ AROLDIS CHAPMAN

In 1980, Major League teams averaged about five strikeouts per game. Today, they're averaging almost eight. One reason is that there are more hitters like Chris Carter who strike out more but also hit more homers.

Another reason is that MLB has more pitchers who can throw serious heat. Cincinnati's Aroldis Chapman has hit 105 miles per hour! As a result of his superfast fastball, he struck out a crazy 51 percent of the batters he faced in the 2014 season.

CAREER STRIKEOUT LEADERS

Rank	Player	Strikeouts
1.	NOLAN RYAN	5.714
2.	RANDY JOHNSON	4.875
3.	ROGER CLEMENS	4.672
4.	STEVE CARLTON	4.136
5.	BERT BLYLEVEN	3.701

▶ RANDY JOHNSON

SINGLE-SEASON STRIKEOUT LEADERS

Rank	Player	Team	Strikeouts	Year
1.	MATT KILROY	ORIOLES	513	1886
2.	TOAD RAMSEY	COLONELS	499	1886
3.	HUGH DAILY	BROWNS. NATIONALS	483	1884
4.	DUPEE SHAW	WOLVERINES. REDS	451	1884
5.	OLD HOSS RADBOURN	GRAYS	441	1884

STAT STARS

CAREER HOME RUNS

762, BARRY BONDS
Pirates and Giants (1986–2007)

SINGLE SEASON HOME RUNS

73, BARRY BONDS
Giants (2001)

CAREER STEALS

1,406, RICKEY HENDERSON
Athletics/Yankees/Padres/Mets/Mariners/Blue Jays/Angels/
Red Sox/Dodgers (1979–2003)

▲ BARRY BONDS

CAREER PITCHING WINS

511, CY YOUNG
Cleveland Spiders/St. Louis Perfectos/Boston Americans/
Red Sox/Cleveland Naps/Boston Rustlers (1890–1911)

SINGLE-SEASON STRIKEOUTS, PITCHING

513, MATT KILROY
Orioles (1886)

SINGLE-SEASON STRIKEOUTS, BATTING

223, MARK REYNOLDS
Diamondbacks (2009)

▲ MATT KILROY

CAREER BATTING AVERAGE

.366, TY COBB
Tigers and Athletics (1905–1928)

SINGLE-SEASON BATTING AVERAGE

.440, HUGH DUFFY
Boston Beaneaters (1894)

CONSECUTIVE GAMES WITH A HIT

56, JOE DIMAGGIO
Yankees (1941)

MOST TIMES HIT BY A PITCH, CAREER

287, HUGHIE JENNINGS
Louisville Colonels/Orioles/Brooklyn Superbas/
Phillies/Tigers (1891–1918)

▲ TY COBB

CONSECUTIVE STOLEN BASES

50, VINCE COLEMAN
Cardinals (September 18, 1988, through July 26, 1989)

CONSECUTIVE SAVES CONVERTED

84, ERIC GAGNE
Dodgers (August 28, 2002, through July 3, 2004)

CONSECUTIVE GAMES PLAYED

2,632, CAL RIPKEN JR.
Orioles (May 30, 1982, through September 19, 1998)

STAT GLOSSARY

batting average (BA)—the ratio of base hits per official times at bat, expressed as a three-digit decimal

earned run average (ERA)—the average number of earned runs a pitcher gives up over nine innings; it is determined by dividing the total number of earned runs scored against him by the total number of innings pitched and multiplying by nine

error—a mistake made by a defensive player; when he doesn't make a play that an average defender would make

fielding independent pitching (FIP)—a measure of a pitcher's effectiveness if he had an average defense behind him; by looking only at strikeouts and walks and home runs allowed—the things that a pitcher controls on his own—it computes a number that looks like ERA

fielding percentage—the percentage of times a defensive player properly handles a batted or thrown ball; it is calculated by the sum of putouts and assists divided by the number of total chances

home run—a hit on which the batter runs around all the bases and scores; most commonly they come on a ball hit out of the park

on-base percentage (OBP)—a measure of how often a batter reaches base; add up the number of times a batter reaches base by hit, walk, or hit by pitch, and divide that sum by the number of times he came to the plate

on-base plus slugging percentage (OPS)—the sum of a player's on-base percentage and his slugging percentage

run batted in (RBI)—a run that a batter causes to score by getting a hit, out, walk, or hit by pitch

save (S)—awarded to a relief pitcher who completes a game that his team wins and he meets one of the following conditions: 1) He enters the game with a lead of no more than three runs and pitches for at least one inning; 2) He enters the game, regardless of the score, with the potential tying run either on base, at bat, or on deck; 3) He pitches for at least three innings

slugging percentage (SLG)—a measure of a hitter's power; it is calculated by dividing the total bases divided by the number of at bats

steal—when a baserunner advances to a base to which he is not entitled; most often a steal occurs when the baserunner runs to the next base while the pitcher is pitching

strikeout (K)—when a batter makes an out by making three strikes in an at-bat; this stat is compiled for batters as well as pitchers

ultimate zone rating (UZR)—how many runs a player saved or gave up through his fielding prowess

walks plus hits per inning pitched (WHIP)—the number of baserunners a pitcher allows on average per inning, not including baserunners who get on by error

win (W)—a win is credited to one pitcher on the winning team in every game; a win is typically awarded to the pitcher who last pitched prior to the half-inning when the winning team took the lead for the last time; a starting pitcher must complete five innings to be eligible for a win